WHICH TO MARS?

By Tisha Hamilton
Illustrated by Jeff LeVan

Modern Curriculum Press

Credits

Illustrations: Jeff Le Van

Computer colorizations by Cathy Pawlowski

Cover and book design by Lisa Ann Arcuri and Agatha Jaspon

ISBN 0-7652-1375-3

Printed in the United States of America

7 8 9 10   08 07 06 05

1-800-321-3106
www.pearsonlearning.com

CONTENTS

**To Mom and Dad,
you're out of this world!**

Chapter 1

Down to Earth

"Mom, Dad, I'm thirsty," Ziggy Mash said. "My water bottle is empty."

Ziggy's mother and father looked at each other. "Well, we still have a long way to go to get home," Mr. Mash said. "The only planet nearby is Earth."

The Mash family were Martians. They were on their way home to Mars from a vacation on Venus.

"I know you don't like Earth," Mrs. Mash said to Mr. Mash. "The people there are so silly when they see Martians. Earth has lots of water. We will make only a short stop."

"Yay!" cried Ziggy. She had never been to Earth.

"OK," Mr. Mash said. He pointed the spaceship toward Earth. In a few minutes they were flying over trees.

"There's a lake," Mr. Mash said. He turned the wheel. Then he flipped a switch.

Suddenly a strong wind pushed the little spaceship. Ka-thunk! It hit a big tree branch. Then the ship spun up in the air. Finally it came down and hit the ground.

"Oh, no!" Mr. Mash said.

Mrs. Mash looked worried. "What if we're stuck on Earth?" she asked. "What will we do?"

Chapter 2

Something in the Sky

Bonnie and Ben Thatcher could hardly wait to eat. They were so hungry. The picnic table was set with paper plates. There was a plate of pickles and a big bottle of ketchup.

Mr. Thatcher turned over a burger on the grill. "We're almost ready," he said.

Whoosh! All of a sudden a big wind blew. Paper plates and napkins went flying. The ketchup bottle fell over.

Bonnie and Ben jumped up to help. Ben caught the plate of pickles. Bonnie ran after the paper plates.

Then Bonnie stopped. "Did you see that?" she asked her brother. "Something just fell out of the sky over by the lake!"

Ben stopped and looked. "I don't see anything," he said.

"It was big and shiny," Bonnie said.

"You're seeing things," Ben laughed.

Chapter 3
Getting Lost

Over by the lake, Ziggy's mother was getting some water. She put it into a special water washer. Soon the water would be safe for the Martians to drink.

Ziggy held out her water bottle. "Wait until I finish," Mrs. Mash said. "Then you can drink the water."

Mr. Mash was lying on the ground under the spaceship. He was looking at the place where the ship hit the tree.

"Dad?" Ziggy asked. "When are we going home? Is our spaceship broken? Do you think you can fix it? Do you need any help?"

"Ziggy, don't get in the way," her mother
said. "Why don't you go get some of those
Earth plants I see growing around here."

"That's a good idea," came the voice of
Ziggy's father from under the spaceship.

"Stay close by," Ziggy's mother said.

Ziggy began to pick flowers and leaves.
There were some lovely yellow flowers near
the water. Ziggy took some.

There were some beautiful blue flowers a
few feet away. Ziggy took some.

There were some pretty purple flowers
near a big tree. Ziggy took some.

Ziggy's hands were full of flowers. Finally Ziggy looked up from the ground.

She could not see the spaceship. She could not see the lake. Ziggy was lost on Earth!

Chapter 4

Smells Like Home

Bonnie and Ben were still chasing paper plates and napkins. Their search took them closer and closer to the woods.

Ziggy smelled something familiar. She followed the smell. Her search took her closer and closer to Bonnie and Ben.

Bonnie reached into a bush to grab the last napkin. Her hand touched something soft and warm.

Ziggy reached into a bush to push a branch back. Her hand touched something soft and warm.

Bonnie and Ziggy yelled at the same time.

"It's a monster!" cried Bonnie.

"I am not!" yelled Ziggy. "I'm a Martian. You're the monster!"

Ben and Bonnie stared. Ziggy stared back.

"A Martian!" said Ben.

"What should we do?" asked Bonnie. "Should we take her home?"

Ziggy's eyes filled with tears. She began to make a honking sound. Ziggy was crying.

"I want my mom and dad," she sobbed. Then she turned gray and fell down.

"I'll stay here," Ben said. "Bonnie, go get Mom and Dad."

Chapter 5

The Care of Martians

Bonnie ran home as fast as she could.

She ran into the yard, huffing and puffing.

"Mom, Dad, come quick!" she yelled.

"What's all the fuss?" Mrs. Thatcher asked.

"There's a Martian in the woods. She needs help," Bonnie said.

"What are you talking about?" Mr. Thatcher said.

"Just come with me," Bonnie said.

Mr. and Mrs. Thatcher went with Bonnie to the woods. They were very surprised to see a small Martian on the ground.

When Ziggy woke up, she saw four Earth people. "I'm hungry," she said.

The Thatchers carried Ziggy to their backyard. Ben handed her a hamburger.

"Yuck!" Ziggy said. "It smells like rocket fuel."

"I don't think she eats the same kind of food we do," Mr. Thatcher said.

"She said something about her mom and dad earlier," Ben said.

"Then we had better find her parents fast," said Mrs. Thatcher. "They must be worried."

"My parents will be so upset," Ziggy cried. "When I smelled rocket fuel, I thought it was my spaceship. I didn't know it was your food."

"That thing I saw go down by the lake must have been their spaceship," Bonnie said. Now Ben believed her.

Chapter 6

Happy Families

The Thatchers put Ziggy in their van. They began to drive to the lake.

"Doesn't this thing fly?" Ziggy asked. She was still very gray.

"No, it only moves on the ground," Ben explained.

"I hope we get there in time," Ziggy said.
"I don't want them to leave without me."

When they got to the lake, the spaceship
was still there. When the Mashes saw the van,
they tried to hide.

"Mom, Dad," Ziggy cried, "don't hide.
These Earth people are nice. They are trying
to help me."

"Ziggy!" the Mashes cried when they saw her. "We were so worried about you!"

"I thought you would be upset," Ziggy smiled.

They hugged and kissed. Then Mrs. Mash saw how gray Ziggy was. She gave Ziggy something that looked like a sponge. As soon as Ziggy ate it, she turned pink again.

"Is the spaceship fixed?" Ziggy asked.

"The branch tore open our fuel tank," Ziggy's father said. "I fixed the tear, but not before all the fuel leaked out."

"I don't know how we'll get home," Ziggy's mother sighed.

"I have an idea," Ziggy said. She talked to her parents and the Thatchers. Then the Thatchers hooked the spaceship to their car. The Mashes and the Thatchers got in. They were all going to a backyard barbecue.

They soon found out that Ziggy was right. Hamburgers made good Martian rocket fuel.

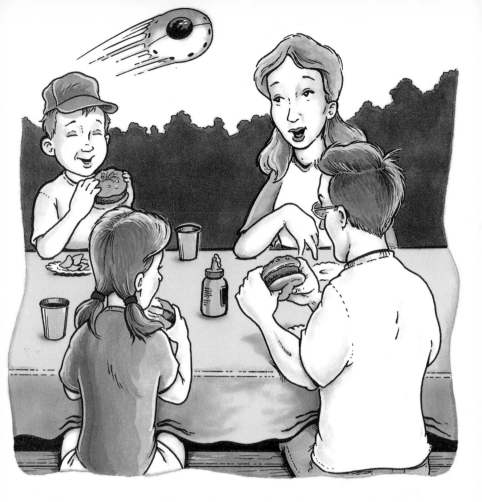

Everyone took turns putting burgers in the fuel tank.

"At last we get to eat," Ben said.

"At last we get to go home," said Ziggy as the spaceship took off. She waved the pickles in her hands. They were the best souvenirs to take home to Mars.

GLOSSARY

barbecue   [BAR bih kyoo] an outdoor cookout; food cooked outdoors over a fire

familiar   [fuh MIHL yur] well-known

fuel   [fyool] a material that gives power to a car or a rocket

leaked   [leekt] came out by accident, as liquid out of a container

rocket   [RAH kut] a long tube that carries things into outer space

souvenir   [soo vuh NIHR] something that reminds a person of something, usually from a trip

sponge   [spunj] a material full of holes that can soak up a lot of liquid

vacation   [vay KAY shun] a trip to have fun